Curriculum Visions

Exploring ancient Greece

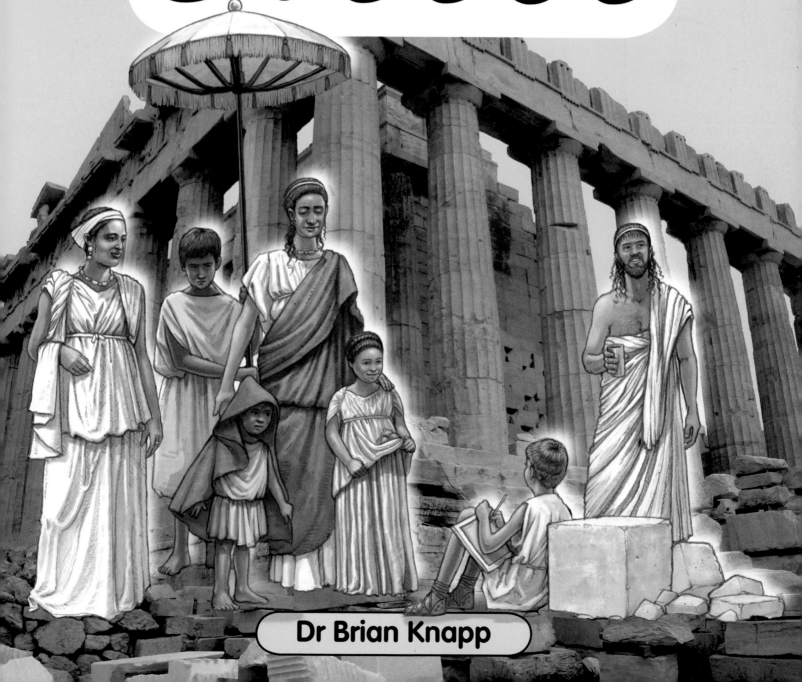

Dr Brian Knapp

World history

Ancient Greeks

3000 BC	2000 BC	1000 BC

Ancient Egyptians (3000–332 BC)

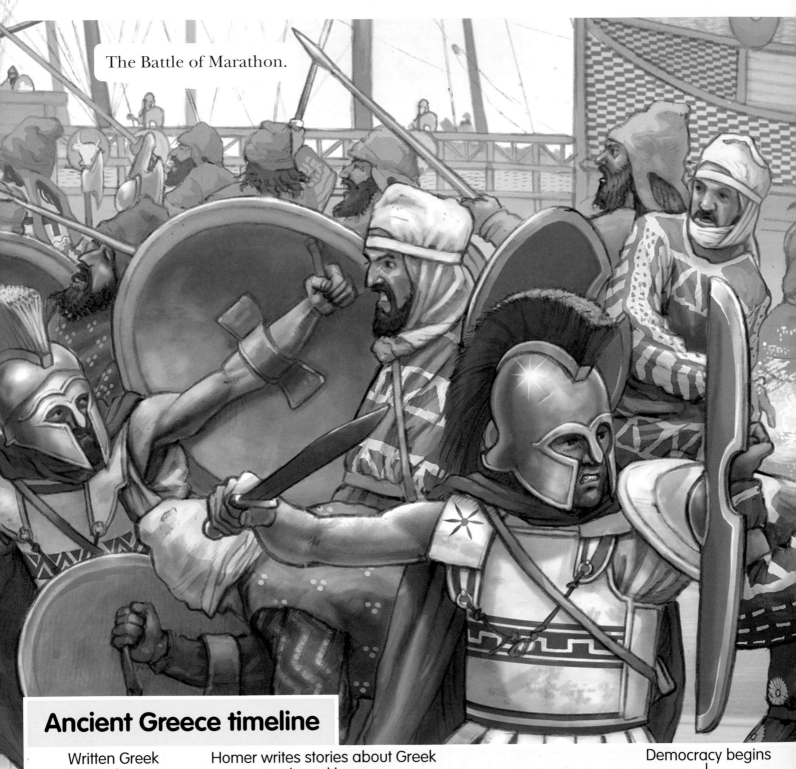

The Battle of Marathon.

Ancient Greece timeline

Written Greek
history begins

Homer writes stories about Greek
gods and heroes

Democracy begins

800 BC	700 BC	600 BC	500 BC

The first
Olympic Games

Coins first used

The Battle of Marathon

The Battle of Salam

(800–146 BC)

0   1000 AD   2000 AD

Anglo-Saxons (450–1066)

Tudors (1485–1603)

Victorians (1837–1901)

Romans (700 BC–476 AD)

Vikings (800–1066/1400)

Contents

Look up the **bold** words in the glossary on page 32 of this book.

Parthenon is built

Alexander the Great builds his empire

First Roman victories over Greece

400 BC   300 BC   200 BC   100 BC

Athens surrenders to Sparta

The Battle of Issus

Greece becomes part of the Roman empire

Meet the ancient Greeks

Greece is a country in Europe. The people who live there are called Greeks. They all speak the language called Greek. In this book you will read about people living in Greece nearly 3,000 years ago.

They are known today as the ancient Greeks.

It is hot and sunny in Greece in the summer and the ancient Greeks used to dress in a way to keep cool. They wore clothes made from square pieces of cloth fastened with brooches and belts.

Here are some people on a sunny day in ancient Greece.

Did you know… ?

- People often wore their hair in ringlets and some women tied up their hair with ribbons.
- The ancient Greeks liked pale skin, too. They tried to keep out of the sunshine.

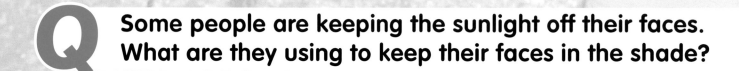

Q Some people are keeping the sunlight off their faces. What are they using to keep their faces in the shade?

What was ancient Greece like?

Ancient Greece was a land of beautiful mountains. The people lived in the valleys between the mountains. They grew olives and grapes and kept goats and sheep. In summer the days were hot, sunny and dry. In winter the days were warm, cloudy and wet.

This photograph shows how mountainous Greece is.

The Greek coast has many sandy bays. This is Marathon, just north of Athens.

Did you know... ?

- The ancient Greeks made olive oil from their olives, and wine from their grapes.
- The weather was too hot for growing wheat in ancient Greece.
- Bread is made from a crop called wheat.
- They traded olive oil and wine for wheat so they could make bread.

Q Can you use a map of the world to find the Mediterranean Sea?

Athens: the largest city

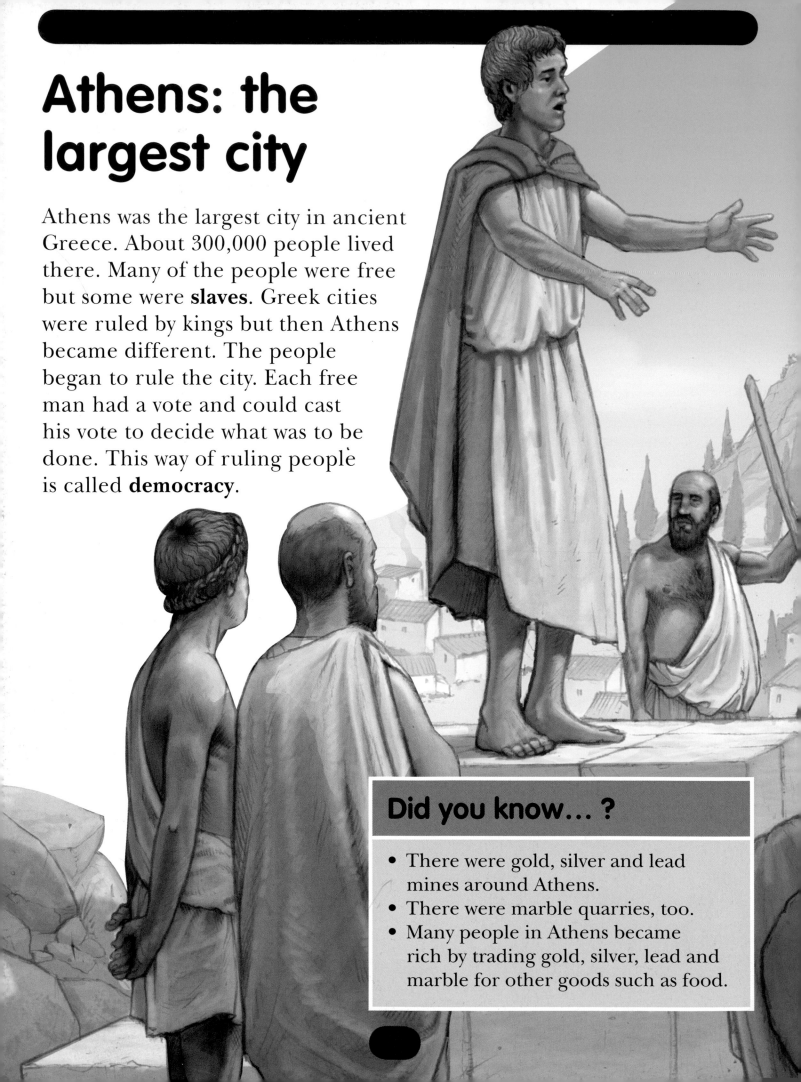

Athens was the largest city in ancient Greece. About 300,000 people lived there. Many of the people were free but some were **slaves**. Greek cities were ruled by kings but then Athens became different. The people began to rule the city. Each free man had a vote and could cast his vote to decide what was to be done. This way of ruling people is called **democracy**.

Did you know... ?

- There were gold, silver and lead mines around Athens.
- There were marble quarries, too.
- Many people in Athens became rich by trading gold, silver, lead and marble for other goods such as food.

The man on the left is telling the others about his ideas for ruling Athens. He is hoping that they will vote for him. Behind the men is a hill called the Acropolis, where temples were built.

Q People sometimes vote in class. What have you voted for in your class?

Alexander the Great – the most famous ancient Greek

Alexander the Great was the most famous leader of the ancient Greeks. All the people in all the Greek cities agreed that he should be their king. He built up a large army and led it into battle. The Greek army fought the armies of other countries and won.

In time the ancient Greeks took over many countries and in this way built up the Greek empire. When the ancient Greeks beat the Egyptians they named a city on the coast of Egypt as Alexandria after Alexander the Great.

The pink shading on this map shows Alexander's empire in 323 BC.

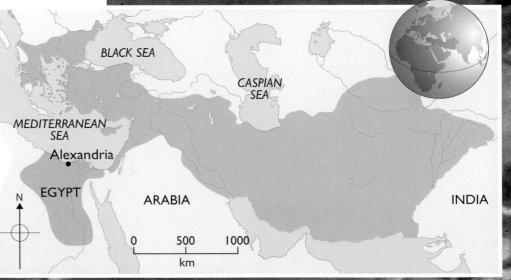

BLACK SEA

CASPIAN SEA

MEDITERRANEAN SEA

Alexandria

N

EGYPT

ARABIA

INDIA

0   500   1000
km

This picture shows the Battle of Issus. Alexander is on the left fighting with King Darius of the Persians who is on the right. Alexander's army won.

Did you know…?

- Alexander was born in 356 BC.
- He became king of Greece in 336 BC, when he was twenty.
- He died in 323 BC, when he was thirty three.

Q Can you use a map from an atlas to see how far Alexander's empire would have reached today?

The Greek gods and heroes

The ancient Greeks believed that their lives were ruled by gods. They thought the gods looked like humans and were very powerful. They thought that when the gods were angry they made bad things happen, so they worshipped the gods by praising them and giving them offerings. The ancient Greeks hoped that the praise and offerings would make the gods happy and let them live in peace.

The ancient Greeks made up stories called **myths**. In a myth there were people called **heroes**, who did amazing things, but they needed the help of gods. Herakles (who we now sometimes know as Hercules) was a hero who was very strong.

This picture shows a statue of the god Apollon.

- A female god was called a goddess.
- The gods and goddesses ruled different parts of life in ancient Greece.
- Apollon ruled over dance and music. He was the god of youth.
- Athena was the goddess of wisdom and war.
- Atlas was the god who held up the sky.

The goddess Athena (left) helps the hero Herakles (centre) temporarily hold up the sky while the god Atlas looks on.

What is the difference between a god and a hero?

Temples to the gods

The ancient Greeks set aside part of the countryside for their gods. These places were called **sanctuaries**. The ancient Greeks' **temples** were built in the sanctuaries. A temple had many tall columns to hold up the roof.

Inside a temple was a large statue of a god or goddess. In front of the statue was a small table where people put their offerings. Behind the statue was a room where the gifts to the god or goddess were stored.

When a person had made an offering to the god or goddess they went outside the temple to an altar and worshipped there.

This is what a temple might have looked like.

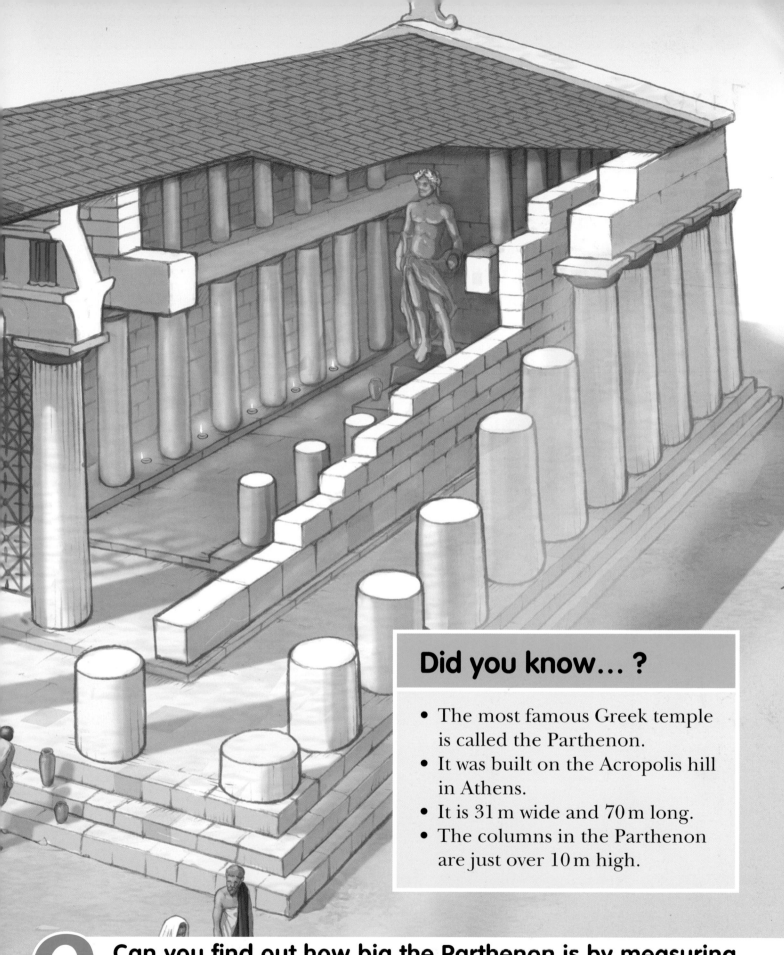

Did you know… ?

- The most famous Greek temple is called the Parthenon.
- It was built on the Acropolis hill in Athens.
- It is 31 m wide and 70 m long.
- The columns in the Parthenon are just over 10 m high.

Q Can you find out how big the Parthenon is by measuring out its length and width outside in the school playground?

The Acropolis

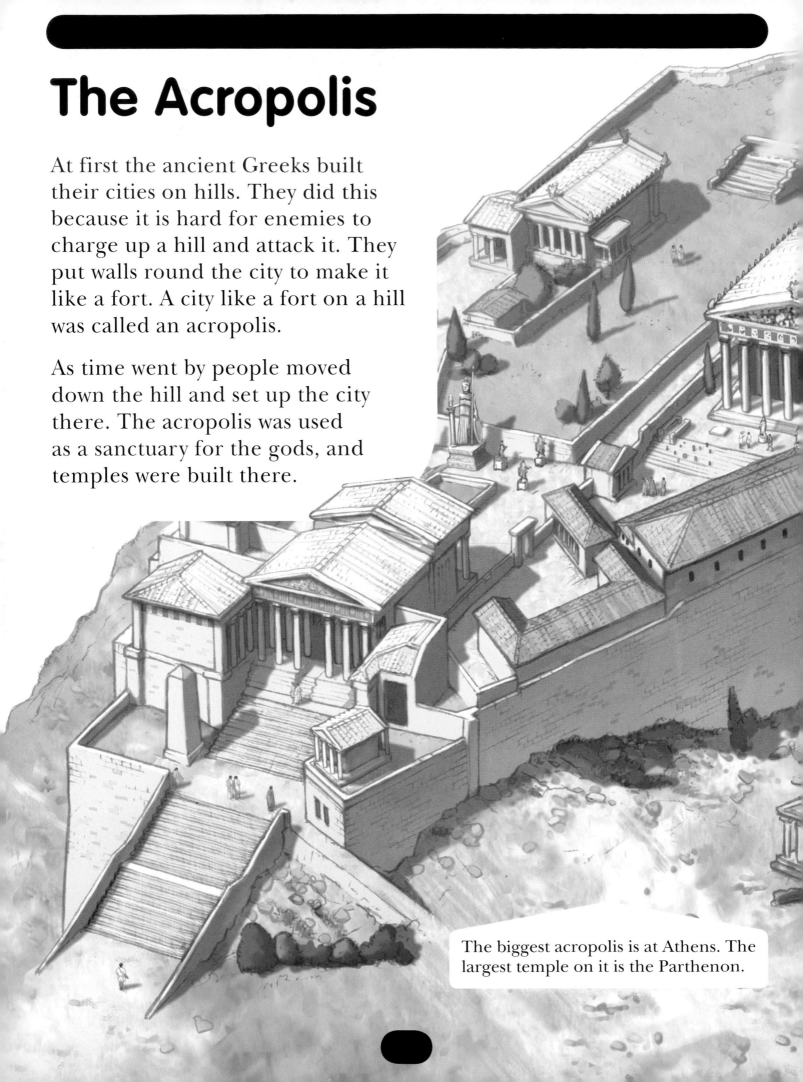

At first the ancient Greeks built their cities on hills. They did this because it is hard for enemies to charge up a hill and attack it. They put walls round the city to make it like a fort. A city like a fort on a hill was called an acropolis.

As time went by people moved down the hill and set up the city there. The acropolis was used as a sanctuary for the gods, and temples were built there.

The biggest acropolis is at Athens. The largest temple on it is the Parthenon.

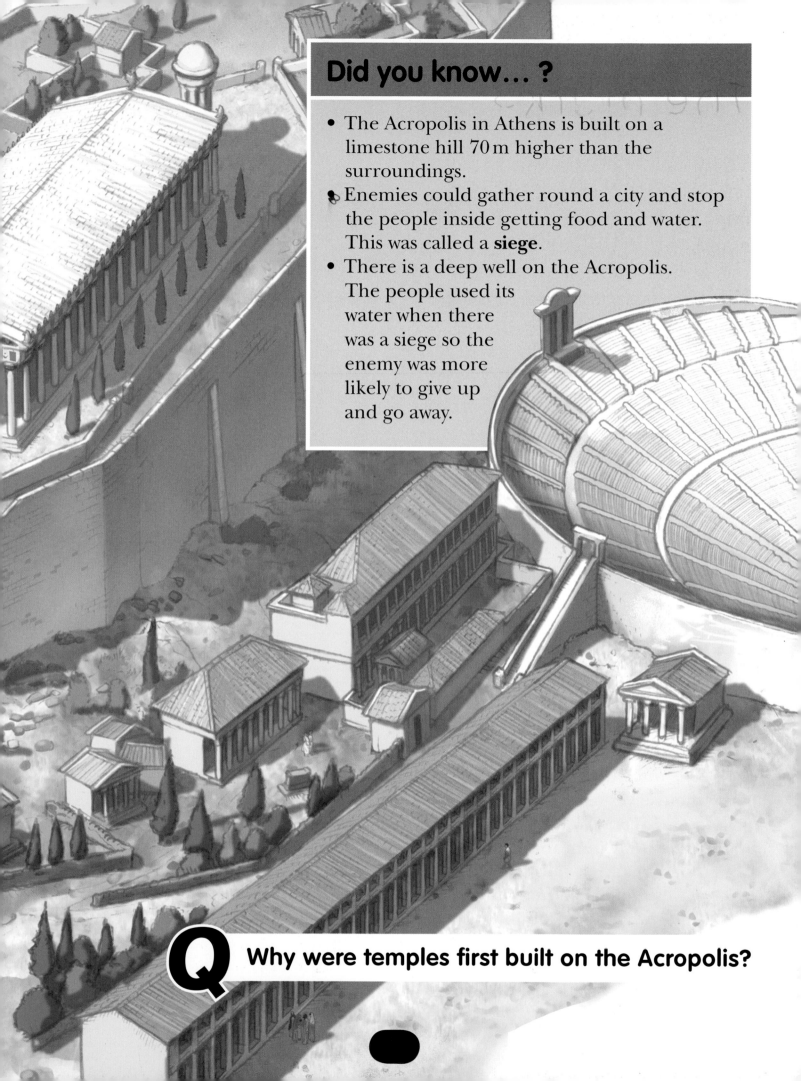

Did you know… ?

- The Acropolis in Athens is built on a limestone hill 70 m higher than the surroundings.
- Enemies could gather round a city and stop the people inside getting food and water. This was called a **siege**.
- There is a deep well on the Acropolis. The people used its water when there was a siege so the enemy was more likely to give up and go away.

Q Why were temples first built on the Acropolis?

Home life

The home of an ancient Greek family had walls made of mud bricks, and a roof made of tiles or thatch. It was built around a courtyard. The courtyard was cool and shady in hot, sunny weather, and kept out the wind in winter. A family would sit in their courtyard in the evening and listen to myths about their heroes.

Did you know... ?

- Women ran the home.
- The house chores and even teaching the children was done by slaves.
- The ancient Greeks washed themselves using olive oil and a bronze scraper.
- The family went to the toilet in pots (chamber pots with lids). The slaves then took the pots out to the fields where the contents were used as fertiliser.

Many houses had just one floor. Some houses, like this one, had two floors.

Q Why was the house built around a courtyard?

The marketplace

In the centre of a city was an open space. It was called an **agora**, which is the ancient Greek for marketplace. Around the agora were rows of shops, the ancient Greeks called **stoa**. Here they could buy food, cloth, jewellery and other things they needed.

The people who shopped were mostly Greek men or their slaves. Greek women did not go to the market very often. If they did, they could not go alone as someone always had to go with them.

When rich people shopped they carried their money in purses in their pockets. When poor people shopped they carried their money in their mouths because they did not have any pockets in their clothes.

In a busy market place in ancient Greece you can see that there are only men buying and selling goods.

Did you know… ?

- In ancient Greek markets, you could buy linen from Egypt, ivory from Africa, and spices from Syria.
- Special offers, such as fresh fish, were called out by the stallholders, just like today.

Q The ancient Greeks stored liquids, such as wine and oil, in jars which had pointed bottoms. The jar was called an amphora. How do you think they got the jars to stand up?

21

The theatre

The theatres in ancient Greece were in the open. They were made in hollows of hillsides. It did not matter that the theatre did not have a roof because in summer the weather was always dry.

There were rows of seats set one above the other. In front of the audience was a circular area for the **chorus** and behind that was the stage.

There were two kinds of play in ancient Greece.

One kind of play was funny and made people laugh. It was called a **comedy**. The second kind of play had a sad ending. It was called a **tragedy**.

Many people helped to make a play. There were actors, singers, dancers and people who played music.

The players wore **masks** to show who they were in the play.

Actors in plays in ancient Greece wore masks like the three actors in the centre of this stage.

Did you know… ?

- Greek theatres could hold up to 15,000 people.
- Dionysus was the god of the theatre.
- Early plays just had one actor.
- Later plays had three actors.

Q **Where do you think the rich people sat?**

The Greeks at war

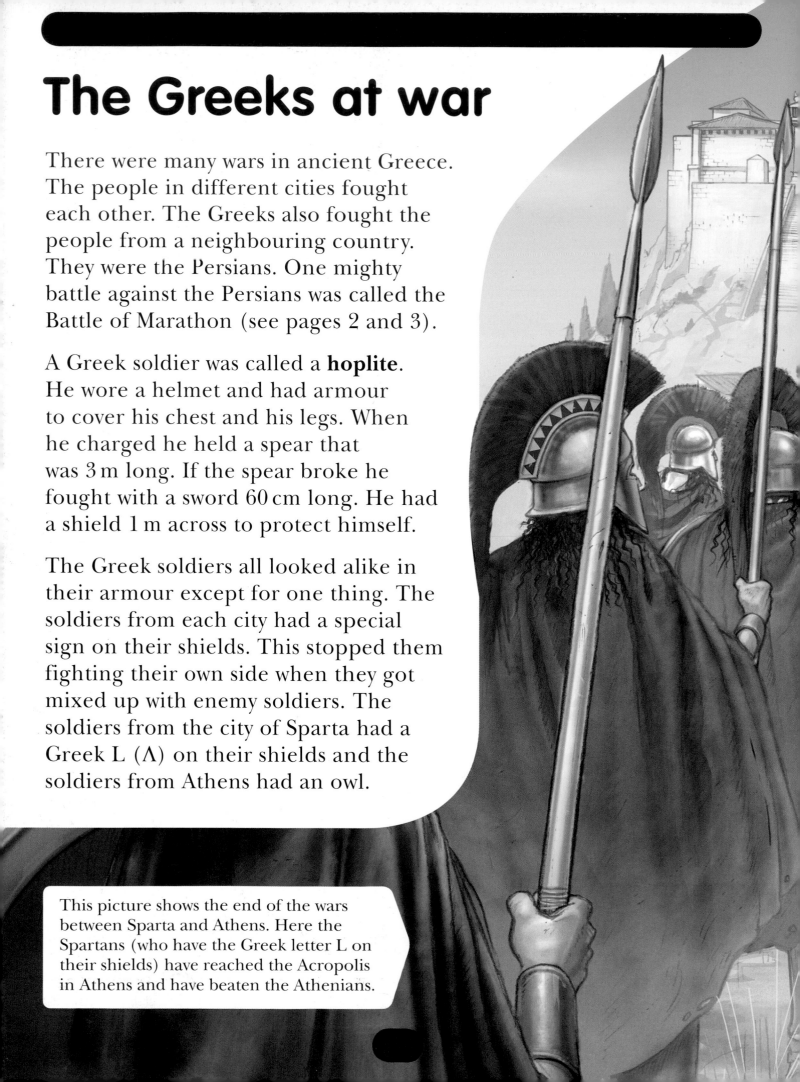

There were many wars in ancient Greece. The people in different cities fought each other. The Greeks also fought the people from a neighbouring country. They were the Persians. One mighty battle against the Persians was called the Battle of Marathon (see pages 2 and 3).

A Greek soldier was called a **hoplite**. He wore a helmet and had armour to cover his chest and his legs. When he charged he held a spear that was 3 m long. If the spear broke he fought with a sword 60 cm long. He had a shield 1 m across to protect himself.

The Greek soldiers all looked alike in their armour except for one thing. The soldiers from each city had a special sign on their shields. This stopped them fighting their own side when they got mixed up with enemy soldiers. The soldiers from the city of Sparta had a Greek L (Λ) on their shields and the soldiers from Athens had an owl.

This picture shows the end of the wars between Sparta and Athens. Here the Spartans (who have the Greek letter L on their shields) have reached the Acropolis in Athens and have beaten the Athenians.

Did you know… ?

- Only free citizens could become hoplites. Their weapons and armour were expensive.
- Poorer people bought cheaper weapons, such as bows and arrows or javelins.
- Very rich people could afford to fight on horseback. A group of riders on horseback makes a cavalry.

Q What sign would you put on your shield?

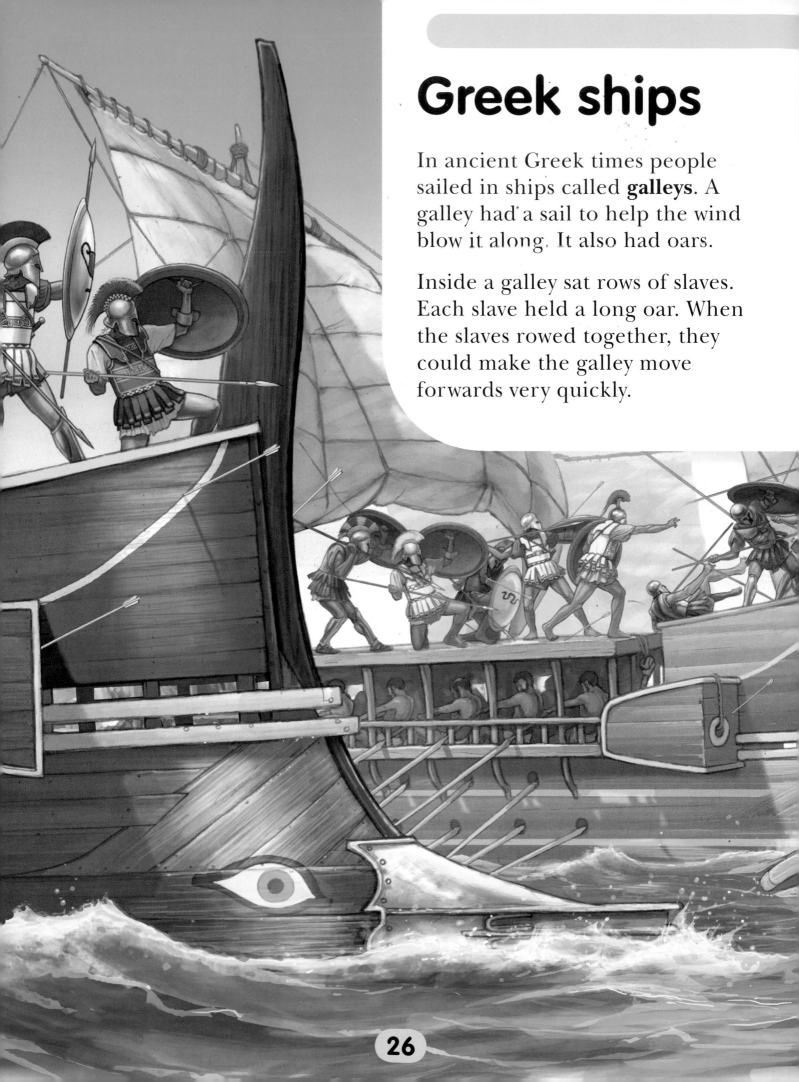

Greek ships

In ancient Greek times people sailed in ships called **galleys**. A galley had a sail to help the wind blow it along. It also had oars.

Inside a galley sat rows of slaves. Each slave held a long oar. When the slaves rowed together, they could make the galley move forwards very quickly.

The biggest galleys had three rows of men on each side. They were called **triremes** because 'tri' means three.

On the front of a trireme was a bronze **battering ram**. When the trireme was travelling fast, the battering ram was used to punch a hole in an enemy ship and sink it. The battering ram could also be used to snap all the oars along one side of an enemy ship.

Did you know...?

- A trireme had up to 170 oarsmen.
- A trireme carried about 30 soldiers called marines.

The most famous sea battle in which the Greeks beat the Persians was called the Battle of Salamis.

Look for the battering ram on the front of the Greek trireme, and the archers on the deck of the Persian ship.

Q **What weapons are being used in this sea battle?**

Olympia and the Games

In ancient Greek times each city held its own Games. In these Games the city's athletes would compete for prizes. But there was nowhere for the athletes from one city to compete against athletes from other cities.

Olympia was a sanctuary for the god Zeus. It was in the countryside away from the main cities. The first time Games were held at Olympia was in 776 BC. At this time all the cities agreed to allow the athletes safe passage across the countryside so they could get to Olympia.

The Games were held inside the sanctuary. A special race track was built, called a **stadion**.

In the earliest Games there was just a single day of races, but over the years more sports were added, such as wrestling and chariot racing, and so the Games lasted for several days.

The winner of each game was given a crown of olive leaves.

The temple of Zeus is in the centre of the picture ①. Behind it is the race track (stadion) ②. In front of it is the gymnasium ③, which has a building on either side where the competitors stayed during the Games.

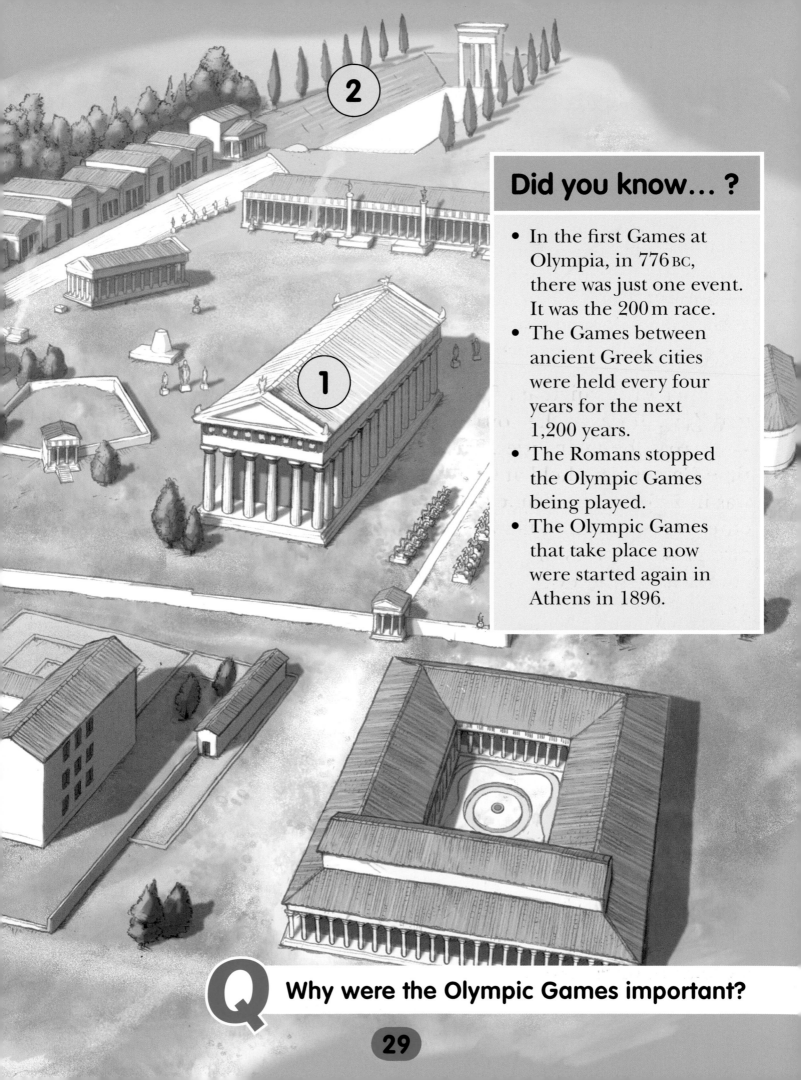

2

1

Did you know… ?

- In the first Games at Olympia, in 776 BC, there was just one event. It was the 200 m race.
- The Games between ancient Greek cities were held every four years for the next 1,200 years.
- The Romans stopped the Olympic Games being played.
- The Olympic Games that take place now were started again in Athens in 1896.

Q Why were the Olympic Games important?

Try these...

Make a chiton

A chiton was a tunic worn by men and women. You can make a chiton simply by wearing a T-shirt for an adult that comes down to your knees, or you can use an old sheet in the following way:

- Make the sheet into a tube by folding it in half and sewing the two free ends together.

- Fasten the top carefully with safety pins but leave spaces for the head and arm holes.

- Put on your chiton and fasten it with a belt.

Make a Greek shield and sword

- Take a large piece of stiff cardboard and cut a circle about 50 cm across. Paint the outside of the shield and add a large letter which stands for your school. Use the Greek alphabet.

- Cut a strip of cardboard and fasten it to the back of the shield so that you are able to get your arm through. Add some string to the rim of the shield by making two holes and tying it in place. This is to help you grip the shield.

- Make a short sword with another piece of cardboard. Cover the blade in kitchen foil to make it shiny.

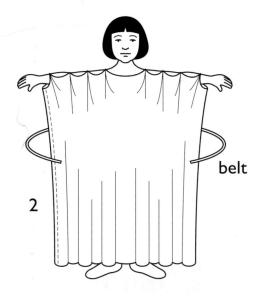

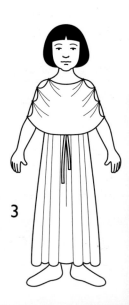

Use the Greek alphabet

English	A	B	C	D	E	F	G	H		I	J	K	L	M
Greek	A	B	Γ	Δ	E	F	Z	H	Θ	I		K	Λ	M

English	N		O	P	Q	R	S	T	U	V	W	X	Y	Z
Greek	N	Ξ	O	Π	Ọ	P	Σ	T		Y	Φ	X	Ψ	Ω

Write a message in Greek using this letter translator. Ask a friend to write it in English using the translator. Challenge your friend to write a Greek message for you to translate back into English.

Make a Greek lunch

The first course

Put pieces of feta cheese in a small bowl and cover with Greek extra virgin olive oil. Add a few stuffed olives.

The second course

Chop up some melon and some peaches and pears. Put them in a bowl and add some grapes. If you do not suffer from a nut allergy you could add some finely chopped almonds. Finally, add the syrup from a can of fruit.

Make a mask

Take a mask you already have and use it as a base for your mask. Make papier mâché from strips of newspaper soaked in a warm, non-allergenic wallpaper paste. Put the strips over the mask face and build up a new one. Cover the new face with white paper and give it a smile or a frown, then paint it.

Make a votive offering

A votive offering was left at a temple by Greek worshippers. Make one out of a lump of black, red or brown Plasticine by shaping it into one of the figures shown here. Alternatively, use self-hardening modelling clay and paint it.

Glossary

agora Greek word for marketplace.

battering ram A weapon used for breaking a hole in a ship or a door.

chorus A group of people who sing together.

comedy A funny play.

democracy A way of getting a ruler of a country by voting.

galley A ship with oars which are rowed by slaves.

hero Someone who people admire because of something important they have done.

hoplite A soldier with armour who fought on foot.

mask A covering that is made for the face.

myth A story about gods and heroes that was not true.

sanctuaries Holy places inside temples or churches.

siege The time when an army surrounds a city and prevents food reaching its people.

slaves People who are owned by other people.

stadion An ancient sports ground with seats for people to watch the games.

stoa A row of covered shops.

temple A building in which one or more gods are worshipped.

tragedy A very sad play.

trireme Ship with three lines of oarsmen on each side.

Index

Curriculum Visions

Curriculum Visions is a registered trademark of Atlantic Europe Publishing Company Ltd.

◆ *Atlantic Europe Publishing*

Curriculum Visions Explorers
This series provides straightforward introductions to key worlds and ideas.

You might also be interested in
Our slightly more detailed book, 'The ancient Greeks'. There is a Teacher's Guide to match 'The ancient Greeks'. Additional notes in PDF format are also available from the publisher to support 'Exploring ancient Greece'. All of these products are suitable for KS2.

Dedicated Web Site
Watch movies, see many more pictures and read much more in detail about the ancient Greeks at:
www.curriculumvisions.com
(Professional Zone: subscription required)

First published in 2007 by Atlantic Europe Publishing Company Ltd
Copyright © 2007 Earthscape

Author
Brian Knapp, BSc, PhD

Consulting Editor
Peter Riley, BSc, C Biol, MI Biol, PGCE

Educational Consultants
JM Smith (former Deputy Head of Wellfield School, Burnley, Lancashire); the Librarians of Hertfordshire School Library Service

Senior Designer
Adele Humphries, BA

Editor
Gillian Gatehouse

Photographs
The Earthscape Picture Library, except *The Granger Collection, New York* p10–11.

Illustrations
Mark Stacey, except p10 *David Woodroffe*

Designed and produced by
Earthscape

Printed in China by
WKT Company Ltd

Exploring ancient Greece
– *Curriculum Visions*
A CIP record for this book is available from the British Library

ISBN 978 1 86214 202 2

This product is manufactured from sustainable managed forests. For every tree cut down at least one more is planted.